I Say! Anyone For Tennis?

Are you an ACTIVE TENNIS-WAG or HAB? That's the wife or girlfriend, or the husband or boyfriend of a keen tennis player who spends all their spare time on the court or in the bar talking about what happened on the court.

Are you a PASSIVE TENNIS-WAG or HAB? That's the wife or girlfriend, or the husband or boyfriend of a passionate tennis-watcher who slobs out on the sofa for the entire Wimbledon fortnight and has the full Sky Sports package to watch all the other tournaments as well.

Are you a WOULD-BE TENNIS-WAG or HAB? That's the intended wife or girlfriend, or the intended husband or boyfriend of a pro tennis player. Imagine the scene - you look appealingly anxious when they're losing and radiant with joy when they're winning … and spend all the money they earn in the meantime!

If you're any of these (or you just want to know what tennis is all about), this book's for YOU!

Sale 5p

The WAGs & HABs
Little Book of Tennis

ЯR
RAVETTE PUBLISHING

ISBN: 978-1-84161-302-4

This edition first published in 2008 by
Ravette Publishing Limited
Unit 3, Tristar Centre, Star Road,
Partridge Green, West Sussex RH13 8RA
United Kingdom

Written by Gordon Volke

Game, Set and Match
to The Tennis-WAG/HAB!

Here's the plan:-

a)   You read this little book from cover to cover.

b)   You learn all you need to know about tennis in a witty and waggish/habbish way.

c)   Then you astonish your other half with your new-found knowledge of the game.

The Result?

You can join them in the bar or on the

sofa, sharing their passion for this strange game.

Order of Play

This book contains an irreverent description of all things tennis including the baffling jargon that TV commentators come out with and think you understand. There's also a bit of history, some vital info about the basics of the game, potted biographies of all the Tennis Gods, some hilarious quotes and *lots* more.

So are you ready?

Play!

HISTORY OF THE GAME

Well, Would You Believe It?

Nobody quite knows where the name 'tennis' comes from. The most likely source is a corruption of the French word 'tenez' which means 'look out, you dozy idiot!'. Early French players were prone to shouting this before they served.

The tennis we're talking about should really be called *Lawn Tennis.* It's a modern form of a very much older game called *Real Tennis* aka *Court Tennis* or *Royal Tennis.*

The Sport of Kings

Nowadays, this title applies to horse racing. In the past, it belonged to Real Tennis. Henry VII, Henry VIII and Charles II were all enthusiastic players and Queen Elizabeth I was a keen spectator.

Being Royalty, they had the space to play this ridiculous game that involved whacking a ball round a huge indoor court with a stone floor and sloping roofs.

Hand Job

The game of Real Tennis began in France around the 12th Century.

Young priests had fun hitting a home-made ball around the cloisters with their bare hands. Later, rackets came to be used instead of hands. Eventually, Real Tennis became a popular game for the very rich in France, England and America. It remains so to this day. Modern players compete for the title 'Champion Of The World'.

(Well, you wouldn't expect anything else, would you?)

Rubber Solution

People tried playing Real Tennis outside, but the cloth-filled ball wouldn't bounce properly on grass. So it wasn't until hollow rubber balls were invented around the 1850s that anything changed. These bounced beautifully on grass and the game of Lawn Tennis was born.

Who Was First?

Nobody's quite sure who invented modern tennis. Major Walter Wingfield from North Wales published an early rule book in 1893.

Then J M Heathcote invented a much superior rubber ball covered in white flannel. And the cricketing authority, the MCC, brought out a more definitive tennis rule book in 1875. Take your pick!

Wimbledon Champs

Lawn tennis really became established in 1877 when the All-England Croquet and Lawn Tennis Club at Wimbledon organised its first Tennis Championship. It was won by Spencer W Gore, a powerful net player with a crafty underarm serve, and the tournament made a small profit for the club. (No change there, then!)

THE SCORING SYSTEM

What The DEUCE Is Going On Here?

Other sports have a straightforward scoring system. In football, you score a small number of goals. In cricket, you score a large number of runs. In rugby, you score tries and conversions. Not so in tennis. It has a weird and wonderful scoring system that is a legacy of its Real Tennis origins. If you don't understand it, here's what it's all about …

You compete for *points*. The player who hits the ball over the net and into the court in such a way that their opponent can't hit it back, wins the point.

The trouble is, each point won does not just score one point. Oh, no! Nothing as simple as that. Each point won scores 15 points! Confused? If not, you soon will be!

If you win two points in a row, you score 30 points. But if you win three points in a row, you only go up to 40. What happened to your other five points? Nobody knows!

If you win the next point after 40 points, you win the *game*.

If the other player does not win any points during the game, he stays on *love*. That means 'nought' in tennis-speak. This has given rise to endless, tedious jokes – example:-

'Never marry a tennis player because love means nothing to them!'
GROAN!

If your opponent does win some points, the game goes like this:-

fifteen - love

You have won the first point.

fifteen - all

Your opponent has won the next point.

fifteen - thirty

Your opponent won the next point too and is now ahead of you.

thirty - all

You have won the fourth point and have caught up.

forty - thirty

You have won the next point and only need one more point to clinch the game.

deuce

Your opponent has won the point instead and you are now equal.

You would expect this to be called *forty-all*, but in fact it's called *deuce*.

The word 'deuce' has nothing to do with the Devil. It comes from the French phrase 'a deux' which means 'at two' or 'you two guys are level, okay?'.

At deuce, you have to win two points in a row to win the game. If you win the first one, you *take the advantage*. If your opponent wins the next point, you go back to *deuce*. If you win it, however, you have gained the magic two-in-a-row and the game is yours.

For the whole of the game that has just been played, one player has been serving (putting the ball into play at the start of each point).

At the end of the game, the service changes over to the other player.

As the match goes on, each player wins a number of games. The one who is first to reach six games, wins the *set*.

Ah! If only it could be that clear. But this is tennis, remember.

If the score becomes five games all, you meet the same 'win double' idea that you had at deuce. Except that you don't!

(Losing the will to live yet? Thought so!)

Up until a few years ago, you had to win two games in a row to clinch a set stuck at five games all. So sets would be won 7–5 or 8–6 etc. The trouble was, if the players were very evenly matched, these sets could go on and on and on. They would end up 15-13 or something silly like that and everyone had died of boredom long ago. So the *tie-break* was introduced.

A tie-break is a ducky little 'set-within-a-set' that acts as a decider. The players serve a couple of points alternately and change ends from time to time to keep it fair. And – HALLELUJAH – a point won here just scores one point. The bottom line is that the first player to reach 7 points wins the tie-break and the set. Except that doesn't always happen!

The final set of most professional tennis matches does *not* have a tie-break at the end. The players must slog it out until one of them gets the two games ahead.

Unless …
You're playing in America! Then it's not the case. Instead, you play a fifth set *super tie-break*. This involves reaching ten points instead of seven and … yes, you guessed it … you have to win by two points if it gets to nine-all!

In most pro tournaments, men play the best of five sets and women play the best of three. So a man has to gain three sets to win the match and a woman two.

When a player needs just one more point to win the final set, they are said to be on *match point*. This moment is very akin to sex in that you need to relax in order to make the big breakthrough and, if you tense up, you tend to lose it.

TENNIS STROKES

Love-leh Volleh!

The 'voice of tennis', the late Dan
Maskell, used to exclaim this when
someone played a winning shot at the
end of a long rally. (The rest of the time,
he said almost nothing – which is why
he's the best TV tennis commentator of
all time.)

But what happens if you don't know
what a volley is? Or a half-volley? Or a
topspin lob? Don't worry! Stroke by
stroke, all is about to be revealed …

Forehand and Backhand

These two shots, known collectively as *groundstrokes*, are the basis of the game. A forehand is played on your right-hand side and a backhand on your left (unless you are left-handed, in which case it's all the other way round). Forehands are easier to play than backhands.

Serve

Every point is started with one of the players throwing the ball into the air and hitting it to the other end of the court. This is called *serving*. The ball must pass over the net without touching it and bounce in the box diagonally opposite the server. You are allowed two serves each time, so if you hit the net or miss the box with the first one, you can try again with the second. Modern pro players have first serves that travel at 100-150 miles per hour!

Smash

This shot is similar to a serve, but you don't throw the ball up yourself. If your opponent is daft enough to hit the ball high into the air, you *smash* it back with terrible ferocity … usually winning the point.

Volley (Forehand or Backhand)

The ball can only bounce once before
you have to hit it. But if you choose to
hit it before it bounces, this is called a
volley. This shot is usually played at the
net and, like the smash, is generally a
point-winner.

Half-Volley

A *half-volley* is when you play the ball
just after it has bounced.
A defensive stroke that often gets
punished by your opponent's next shot.

Drive Volley

This is when you're on the attack. You run forwards and hit the ball early, *driving* it back over the net like a rocket. Can be a spectacular winner ... but it's equally likely to go out!

Lob and Topspin Lob

Hitting the ball over your opponent's head is called a *lob*.
It's quite hard to do if you're playing against someone half-decent because it gives them a chance to blast away a smash. But if you're clever, you can

disguise the shot by putting a lot of spin on it. A good *topspin lob* goes right over your opponent's head in an arc and lands right on the baseline, leaving him flat-footed and open-mouthed with disbelief.

Dropshot

This is a sneaky little shot in which you hit the ball very gently so that it just drops over the net. Your opponent has to run like crazy to reach it. They usually do, so it's a risky manoeuvre.

Stop Volley

Same as a dropshot, only played without the ball bouncing first.
From the net, you plop the ball into a nice empty space and there it dies. Very satisfying!

JOKES

You Cannot Be Serious!

With apologies to John McEnroe for borrowing his most famous line, here's a small selection of tennis-related laughs …

Running through the park one morning, a jogger found a new tennis ball on the grass. Making sure there was no one around, he picked the ball up and slipped it into the pocket of his shorts.

Later, on the way home, he was forced to stop at a pedestrian crossing while the lights changed. A pretty blonde girl standing next to him on the kerb noticed the big bulge in his shorts.

"What's that?" she asked, playfully.

"Tennis ball," panted the jogger.

"Oh, dear," said the blonde. "That must be very painful. I had tennis elbow once …"

Question -
How many tennis players does it take to screw in a light bulb?

Answer -

What do you mean 'it was out?' It was in!

A married couple go to hospital to have their baby delivered.
When they arrive, the doctor says they're trying out a new machine that transfers some of the mother's pain to the father.
"Would you like to try it out?" asks the doctor.
"I'd love to," replies the kind and loving husband.

When the woman goes into labour,
the doctor sets the machine to
10% and asks the man if it hurts.
"No, that's okay," he replies.
So the doctor increases it to 20%.
"Still okay," calls the man.

Bit by bit, the doctor raises the
setting to 50%.
"Can you cope?" he asks.
"Yes," whispers the husband,
gritting his teeth.
So the doctor puts the setting up
again to 75%.
"I c-c-can still take it!" yells the man.
"Give me the whole 100%!"

The doctor does as he's asked and the wife delivers the baby with absolutely no pain at all. As the doctor goes to report this amazing case to the British Medical Council, the couple take their new baby home. And, on their doorstep, they find the wife's tennis coach – dead!

And, finally, this old chestnut that appears in almost every single Christmas cracker…

Why don't fish make good tennis players?

They don't like getting too close to the net!

INFO ABOUT THE COURT

Court Jester

It's not possible to make factual info about a tennis court funny, so it's being sandwiched between two lots of funny stuff. If you're going to become a proper tennis-WAG/HAB, you have to take the rough with the smooth ... okay?

a)   a tennis court is marked out for both singles and doubles play

b)   if you play singles, you only use the inner sidelines - this makes the court measure 23.8 x 8.2 metres (78 x 27 feet)

c) if you play doubles, you include the outer sidelines and this widens the court - it now measures 23.8 x 11 metres (78 x 36 feet)

d) the proper name for the space between these sidelines is the *alley* – but most people call them the *tramlines*

e) the net across the court must be at a height of exactly 0.9 metres (3 feet) at the centre - this is measured with a *stick*

f) the net is held up by *net posts* - these are just over 1 metre (3 feet, 6 inches)

high and must be outside the
playing area

g) the lines at either end of the court
are called the *baselines*

h) the lines across the middle of the
court are called the *service lines* and
the four oblong boxes either side of
the net are the *service boxes*

Okay, you've had enough! On with the
funny stuff!

TENNIS COMMENTATING BLOOPERS

Game For A Laugh

Oh, to be a tennis commentator! It's the tennis-WAG/HAB's dream – getting paid for sitting there and chatting about a match that other people have queued outside for three days to see. But it's not as easy as it looks, if these famous names are anything to go by …

McEnroe has got to sit down and work out where he stands.

Fred Perry

The Gullikson twins here. An interesting pair, both from Wisconsin.

Dan Maskell

Chip Hooper is such a big man that it is sometimes difficult to see where he is on the court.

Mark Cox

Diane – keeping her head beautifully on her shoulders

Ann Jones

The ball boys are marvellous. You don't even notice them. There's a left-handed one over there. I noticed him earlier.

Max Robertson

Zivojinovic seems to be able to pull the big bullet out of the top drawer.

Mike Ingham

He's got his hands on his knees and holds his head in despair.

Peter Jones

It's quite clear that Virginia Wade is thriving on the pressure now that the pressure on her to do well is off.

Harry Carpenter

Martina, she's got several layers of steel out there like a cat with nine lives.

Virginia Wade

Lloyd did what he achieved with that
shot.

Jack Bannister

Strawberries, cream and champers
flowed like hot cakes.

Radio 2 Commentator

She comes from a tennis playing family.
Her father's a dentist.

BBC 2 Commentator

FAMOUS TENNIS PLAYERS – PART 1

Gods of the Dim and Distant Past

To be a proper tennis-WAG/HAB, you need to know lots of famous players and drop their names into conversations to increase your court-cred.

These are the important heroes from the early years …

Fred Perry
Won Wimbledon three times in a row (1934-36) … the last British male player ever to do so!

Bunny Austin
Perry's doubles partner. Pioneered the wearing of short trousers for playing

tennis. Died August 26th, 2000.

Little Mo
Maureen Connolly was a sensational
American player in the early Fifties. She
was American champion at only 16 and
won Wimbledon three times. Her career
was cut short by a riding accident.

Althea Gibson
Her achievement is best summed up in
her own words …

> "Here stands before you a Negro
> woman, raised in Harlem, who went
> on to become a tennis player …
> champion, in fact, the first black
> woman champion of this world."

Rod Laver
Small, super-fit Australian player of the late Fifties and early Sixties. Other legendary Australian names of the same period were *Frank Sedgeman, Lew Hoad* and *Ken Rosewall.'*

Angela Mortimer, Ann Jones and *Christine Truman*
British women players who won or were finalists at Wimbledon. They still work as commentators.

Billie Jean King
A fierce, bespectacled American who won Wimbledon three times (1966-68). Worked hard to raise the profile of women's tennis.

TENNIS TERMS

Coming to TERMS with Tennis

Right! Time to get down to the nitty-gritty!

Any tennis-WAG/HAB worth their sweatbands needs to know and understand all the technical terms to do with tennis. So study carefully and memorise, but don't eat the book because you haven't finished reading it yet.

Ace

A service that cannot be returned. (The ball needs to remain completely untouched for it to be a proper ace.)

Approach Play

a) A pick-up technique, involving hanging around in the right spot and getting noticed, employed by ambitious tennis-WAGs/HABs in clubs on a Saturday night.

b) On court, moving towards the net in order to play a volley and try to win the point.

Australian Doubles Formation

This is a weird practice sometimes used during a game of doubles. Both partners stand on the same side of the court when one of them is serving. Other than confusing the opposition, what this actually achieves remains a mystery.

Ball Toss

Tossing well is an important skill to master and tennis players practice it a lot, especially the men. Away from the showers, it involves throwing the ball up into the air ready to serve it.

Baseline Play

Some players don't risk going up to the net to make a winning shot with a volley. Instead, they stand behind the baseline and keep hitting the ball backwards and forwards, backwards and forwards. It makes for … YAWN … a fascinating match … SNORE!

Blue Collar Tennis

Nothing to do with washing powder! This phrase means that a player is under pressure (ie. losing) and needs to work extra hard to start winning points and catch up.

Breaking Serve and Breaking Back

Serving is very important in tennis. It gives the player a considerable advantage. So, in most matches, the games *go with serve*. In other words, they are won by the person serving. But if the server's opponent wins the game, that is called *breaking the serve*. Having just lost your serve, it's vital to inflict the same punishment on your opponent and break their serve in the next game *(breaking back)*.

Clay Court

Lawn tennis is seldom played on grass.
(What else would you expect?) Most of
the time, it's played on asphalt – that's
the surface in your local park. It's also
played on other all-weather surfaces and
indoors, on wood. The most popular
surface, however, is a powdery red or
green shale made of crushed brick. This
is what you find in most tennis clubs and
at the French Open Championships. This
is called a *clay* court.

Continental Grip

There are various styles of holding the racket and this is one of them. Others are the *Western Grip, Eastern Grip* and some *semi* variations of all of them. Please don't bother with any of this stuff because …

   a) it's too technical

   b) it's mind-blowingly boring

Crosscourt Shot

Hitting the ball *crosscourt* describes a shot that goes diagonally across the net to the opposite corner. It's a rare instance of a tennis term making sense and meaning what you'd expect.

Double Fault

This is when *both* your services go into the net or out and you lose the point. Most pro players can manage to get one of their two serves into play, so double-faulting is a sign that they're nervous or seriously off form, or both.

Donut/Bagel

The term for losing a set without winning a game ie. 6-0 to your opponent (the donut/bagel referring to the 0).

Double Bagel

The term for losing *two* sets without winning a game in either of them.

Foot Fault

When you serve, you must stand behind the base line. If you tread on the line or over it, you incur a *foot fault*. The beefy lady line judge will then bellow, "FAULT !!" and that service is scrapped. Like double-faulting, foot faulting is a beginner's error and it's something any decent player should be ashamed of.

Footwork

Good players are said to have good footwork. This means they get into position to play each shot with the maximum power. There are lots of footwork terms like *side-step*, *cross-step* and *tango*, but don't go there either. It's the realm of the tennis coach or tennis nerd.

Follow Through

What are you like? This has nothing to do with an embarrassing farting accident. *Following through* means completing a stroke (usually a groundstroke) with an elaborate flourish.

It makes a huge difference to the speed, length and direction of the ball.

Golden Set

Believe it or not, there has only been one of these in the history of professional tennis (so far). It means winning a set without your opponent gaining a *single point* against you. It was achieved by an American player, Bill Scanlon, during a first round match in a tournament in Florida in February 1983.

Grand Slam

The Australian Open, French Open, Wimbledon and US Open are the world's four major tennis championships. To win them all, you gain *the Grand Slam*. So they are known as *Grand Slam* tournaments. *(See pages 79– 84 for further details.)*

Gut

Posh rackets are strung with gut, a springy string made from the innards of animals. It snaps easily, so cheaper rackets use nylon or other synthetic strings instead.

Head

This is the top of the racket where the strings are. (What were you thinking?)

Inside-Out Forehands and Backhands

Also known as *running round* your forehand or backhand, these terms mean taking a shot in a way that plays to your strengths. For example, if you have a strong forehand and a weak backhand, it will suit you to play as many forehands and as few backhands as possible. So, when the ball is played to your backhand side, you move right round and hit it with a forehand stroke instead of the expected backhand. (It's not a particularly clever strategy because you leave lots of wide open spaces on the court and your opponent can hit the ball into them with his next shot.)

Kick Serve

A special type of service, with lots of heavy spin, that makes the ball change direction and kick high into the air when it bounces on the other side of the net. Bamboozles your opponent.

Let

If a ball clips the net after it has been served, it cannot be played, even if it lands properly in the service box. You have to play a *let* which means that the serve is taken again. Sometimes this call is changed to *net*, but that is not strictly correct.

Line Judges

These are people who sit around the edge of the court, deciding which balls are in and which are out. Those you see at Wimbledon look like rejects from a bowls tournament and lead you to believe in life-after-death.

Long Line

Hitting the ball straight along one of the sidelines. Also referred to as *hitting down the line*.

Moon Ball

This is a high lob, played during one of those long, boring baseline exchanges mentioned earlier, to break up the rhythm and change the game.

No-Man's Land

The area between the baseline and the service line. It's the wrong place to stand because shots are very difficult to play here.

Not Up

You are dreadful! No, this isn't a male problem that needs viagra … it's the call the umpire makes if the ball bounces twice before being hit.

Passing Shot

A winning shot that passes your opponent at the net.

Playing the Percentages

This makes good sense in the permanently peculiar world of tennis. Each game has the same number of points to be won. So if you run yourself ragged trying to win a very long rally, you still only gain one point. It's better to concentrate on the other 'everyday' points - particularly those you're likely to win easily.

Ready Position

Players ready position ... knees slightly
bent, weight leaning forwards,
racket held up in front of body.

Rally

The ball being hit backwards and
forwards over the net a number of times
... *or* ... the word 'really' being spoken in
the Royal Box at Wimbledon.

Seeding

This is a cunning ploy to prevent the top
players meeting each other too early
during a tournament and knocking each

other out. They are graded so that, provided they beat the lesser players during the early rounds, they only play each other during the later stages.

Show Court

The Centre Court, Court No. 1 and Court No. 2 are Wimbledon's show courts. Only the big stars play on them. Lesser mortals have to be content with the *outside courts* – unless they keep winning … then they will find themselves on one of the show courts for the quarter-finals, semi-finals and final of the competition.

Unforced Errors

Losing points by your own mistakes
rather than pressure from your
opponent.

FAMOUS TENNIS PLAYERS – PART 2

Gods of the Golden Age

During the Seventies, Eighties and Nineties, there were some *fantastic* players whose names are forever enshrined in tennis folklore. To achieve full tennis-WAG/HAB status, you need to know them all …

Arthur Ashe

The first male Black Wimbledon champion. A cool customer who meditated between games. Also remembered for his work for good causes.

Margaret Smith

A stocky Australian who won more Grand Slam titles than anyone else … 24 in all!

Virginia Wade

The last British tennis player to win Wimbledon. Her triumph came in 1977, the year of the Queen's Golden Jubilee. Presented with her trophy by the Sovereign herself, our Ginny made it quite clear who the crowd should be cheering.

Jimmy Connors

A dynamic American who debunked the restrained image of the tennis player, clowning around and behaving like a passionate human being on court.

Chris Evert

A willowy blonde American with rock solid groundstrokes who wore her opponents down by playing most of her shots from behind the baseline.

Martina Navratilova

Evert's great rival and perhaps the biggest name in women's tennis. Won Wimbledon for the first time in 1978 and went on to win it a further breathtaking *eight times* in the Eighties and Nineties (plus countless other titles). Retired September 2006.

Bjorn Borg

A Swede who played amazing topspin groundstrokes. Won Wimbledon five times in a row (1976-80). Now the head of a very successful company selling underpants.

John McEnroe

Borg's great rival – the matches between them were legendary. Famous for his bad temper, swearing and on-court antics. A breathtaking player with nerves of steel. Now very involved with UK tennis and a top BBC commentator.

Boris Becker

A German. At 17, the youngest male player ever to win Wimbledon.

Pete Sampras

Known as 'Pistol Pete' for his habit of blasting away the opposition. He is also known for winning Wimbledon a staggering *seven* times (1993-95 and 1997-2000) … and being very hairy.

Steffi Graf

A powerful German player who took Martina Navratilova's crown in 1988 and eventually won Wimbledon a further six times. Married Andre Agassi.

Andre Agassi

Always the crowd's favourite, a round-faced, good-natured power-player with a bald head. Won Wimbledon once in 1992.

FUNNY TENNIS QUOTES

You Can Quote Me On This!

By now, you trainee tennis-WAGs/HABs should be realising that tennis, in Jimmy Greaves' immortal phrase about football, is "a funny old game". So it should come as no surprise that there are a plethora of witty quotes on all aspects of the sport.

Here are some of the best …

In tennis, the addict moves about a hard rectangle and seeks to ambush a fuzzy ball with a modified snow-shoe.

Elliot Chaze

The serve was invented so that the net could play.

Bill Cosby

"Good shot", "bad luck" and "hell" are the five basic words to be used in a game of tennis – though these, of course, can be slightly amplified.

Virginia Graham

A traditional fixture at Wimbledon is the way the BBC TV commentary box fills up with British players eliminated in the early rounds.

Clive James

If Borg's parents hadn't liked the name,
he might never have been Bjorn.

Marty Indik

Everyone thinks my name is Jerry Laitis
and they call me Mr Laitis. What can you
do when you have a name that sounds
like a disease?

Vitas Gerulaitis

An otherwise happily married couple
may turn a mixed doubles game into a
scene from 'Who's Afraid Of Virginia
Woolf?'.

Rod Laver

If someone says tennis is not feminine, I say screw it!

Rosie Casals

Ladies, here's a hint. If you're up against a girl with big boobs, bring her to the net and make her hit backhand volleys. That's the hardest shot for the well-endowed.

Billie Jean King

(After beating 14 year old Jennifer Capriati to winning a car)
It's just as well that I won because, if Jennifer won, she couldn't drive it anyway.

Martina Navratilova

Wimbledon

"Wimbledon is the oldest, the most famous and certainly the most prestigious tennis tournament in the world."

John Parsons
- World Encyclopedia of Tennis

* Third Grand Slam tournament of the year.
* June - July
* All England Tennis and Croquet Club, Wimbledon, London SW19.
* Grass courts (very fast).
* Centre Court and No. 1 Court are world famous. The other show

court, No. 2 Court, is known as 'the graveyard of champions' because so many have lost there when nobody was watching.

The United States Open

* Fourth and final Grand Slam.
* August - September
* Hard court surface.
* Played at (ready for this?) *The USTA Billie Jean King National Tennis Centre* at *Flushing Meadows, Corona Park, Queen Borough, New York City.* (Phew! Most people just call the place Flushing Meadows.)

*   Differs from the other three Grand
       Slams in the way that matches are
       concluded. The Americans play a
       fifth set tie-break.

The Davis Cup

Different nations compete for this. It's
organised in various *zones* (which you
don't need to understand) and the
matches played are called *rubbers*. Four
male players represent each country,
playing four singles matches and one
doubles. Some top players consider it a
great honour to take part in the Davis
Cup. Others think it's a drag. They're
making too much money and having too
much fun on the pro circuit!

FAMOUS PLAYERS – PART 3

Today's Tennis Gods

These are the names you need to know from the modern game to complete your tennis-WAG/HAB education.

Roger Federer
Swiss. Currently winning almost everything with effortless ease. Possibly the greatest tennis player *ever*.

Tim Henman
Has carried the hopes of the British public for many years, but never reached a Wimbledon final. Often the butt of many unfair jokes. Has done very nicely out of his career, thank you very much.

Andrew Murray
The new British hopeful. Scottish. The English crowd will always adopt a hero if they haven't got one of their own.

Anna Kournikova
Not much good at tennis, but *what* a babe! Now models bras with the slogan … "Only the ball should bounce".

Maria Sharapova
Russian. Another stunner, but one who can really play. Has won three Grand Slam titles … Wimbledon in 2004, US Open in 2006 and Australian Open in 2008.

Lleyton Hewitt
Australian. Usually there or thereabouts in the big tournaments.

Won Wimbledon in 2002.

Andy Roddick
American. Another player regarded as a genuine contender for any title. Beaten Wimbledon finalist 2004 and 2005.

Venus Williams and Serena Williams
The Williams sisters are a tennis phenomenon. Their awesome strength and power just blows the opposition away. Often play each other in the finals of tournaments. Have won Wimbledon twice each.

Rafael Nadal
A young Spanish newcomer. Beaten Wimbledon finalist in 2006. One to watch for the future.

QUIZ

Hawk-Eye Instant Replay

This is the latest technical gismo employed to stop disputed line calls currently on trial at the US Open. It's also an apt title for this little quiz to see if you've remembered anything of what's been said.

Answer the subtly humorous questions. Then check your score against the score-rating chart. Have you gained your tennis-WAG/HAB status?

1. With what do you associate the name *Flushing Meadows*?

   a) the US Open
   b) a self-watering grass court
   c) toilets

2. You have to gain nine points to win a normal tie-break.

   a) true
   b) false

3. What was Spencer W Gore the first person to do in 1877?

   a) play tennis in shorts
   b) win Wimbledon
   c) read to the end of a Dickens novel

4. Whereabouts on the court is *No-man's Land*?

5. What is the proper name for a score of 40 - 40?

6. What is the first name of the nine-times Wimbledon champion and tennis superstar, Ms Navratilova?
   a) Martini
   b) Martinique
   c) Martina

7. What is the everyday name for the long, straight lines down either side of the court?
   a) the grid
   b) the tramlines
   c) the bus lanes

8. Who was known as 'the voice of tennis'?
   a) Ian Paisley
   b) John Motson
   c) Dan Maskell

9. Rearrange these letters to spell the part of a monastery or cathedral where Real Tennis was first played …
   S R L C T I E O S

10. What do tennis matches during the Davis Cup and condoms have in common?

11. How old was Boris Becker when he first won Wimbledon in 1985?

   a) 7
   b) 17
   c) 77

12. Complete the name of the line that runs across the middle of a tennis court …

   The s - - - - - - line

13. What do you have to do to produce a *kick serve*?

   a) put a lot of heavy spin on it
   b) hit the ball very hard
   c) kick the ball

14. Where and when is the Australian Open played every year?

15. Which one of these three Wimbledon champions is the odd one out and why?

   a) Pete Sampras
   b) John McEnroe
   c) Roger Federer

Answers

1. a) the US Open
2. False - you have to gain seven points
3. b) win Wimbledon
4. *No-man's Land* is in the middle of the court
5. Deuce
6. c) Martina
7. b) the tramlines
8. c) Dan Maskell
9. CLOISTERS
10. they are both known as *rubbers*
11. b) 17
12. the service line
13. a) put a lot of heavy spin on it
14. in Melbourne in January
15. b) John McEnroe - the other two always behave impeccably on court

Score Ratings

0 – 5 points
Er … words like 'whitewash' and 'double-bagel' come to mind. Not to worry … see the next page for your escape.

6 – 10 points
Nobody remembers the losing Wimbledon finalist, but never mind. You tried hard and that's the thing. If you're determined to succeed, you could always do it all again.

11- 15 points
Game, set and match to you! Congratulations. You've passed with flying colours and can consider yourself a qualified tennis-WAG/HAB.

CONCLUSION

So there we are. You've become a tennis-WAG/HAB ... or you haven't!

If you haven't, here's your get-out clause ...

1. Enthusiastically cheer your other half with a degree of style.

2. Wear designer sunglasses.

3. Ensure your tan is always topped up.

4. Dress: relaxed sports gear for the HABs ... stylish tops and funky jewellery for the WAGs.

5. Don't go without your hi-tech mobile, so you can take pictures of your partner on court.

6. Drive the latest off-roader or sportscar.

7. Always be aware of the paparazzi and make sure you have a pose ready at all times.